Our Nation's Pride

Ellis Island

By Karen Latchana Kenney
Illustrated by Judith A. Hunt

Content Consultant:
Richard Jensen, PhD
Author, Scholar, and Historian

visit us at www.abdopublishing.com

Published by Magic Wagon, a division of the ABDO Group, 8000 West 78th Street, Edina, Minnesota, 55439. Copyright © 2011 by Abdo Consulting Group, Inc. International copyrights reserved in all countries. All rights reserved. No part of this book may be reproduced in any form without written permission from the publisher.

Looking Glass Library™ is a trademark and logo of Magic Wagon.

Printed in the United States of America, North Mankato, Minnesota.
092010
012011

Text by Karen Latchana Kenney
Illustrations by Judith A. Hunt
Edited by Melissa Johnson
Interior layout and design by Becky Daum
Cover design by Becky Daum

Library of Congress Cataloging-in-Publication Data
Kenney, Karen Latchana.
  Ellis Island / by Karen Latchana Kenney ; illustrated by Judith A. Hunt.
     p. cm.
  Includes index.
  ISBN 978-1-61641-150-3
  1. Ellis Island Immigration Station (N.Y. and N.J.)—History—Juvenile literature. 2. United States—Emigration and immigration—History—Juvenile literature. I. Hunt, Judith A., 1955- ill. II. Title.
  JV6484.K46 2011
  304.8'73—dc22
                              2010013995

Table of Contents

The First Stop

From a boat in New York Harbor, people see an island. Many old buildings rise from its shores. The boat stops by a big red-and-white stone building.

The visitors have arrived at Ellis Island. This was once the first stop in the United States for many immigrants. These people came to America to start new lives.

4

Gateway to America

In the late 1800s, life was hard for many people in Europe. Many came to America because they wanted a better life.

There were rules to enter the United States, though. The government built a station at Ellis Island. Immigrants had to pass through the station before they could enter their new country. This way, the government could be sure the immigrants followed the rules. This is why Ellis Island is known as the Gateway to America.

6

The Island's Name

Long ago, Ellis Island was a bare, sandy beach. Seagulls flapped overhead. American Indians called the island *Kioshk*, which means "Gull Island." Then, it was called Little Oyster Island for the oysters found nearby.

Samuel Ellis bought the island in the 1770s. He named it after himself. When the government bought the island in 1808, the name stayed.

The First Station

The government had plans for Ellis Island.

It wanted to build a station there for immigrants.

In 1890, workers added dirt and sand to make the

island bigger. They made buildings out of wood.

On January 1, 1892, the station opened. An

Irish girl named Annie Moore was the first to come

through.

A Big Fire

On June 15, 1897, a big fire broke out on

the island. The main building burned down.

The government decided to build a new, fireproof

station. This time, the buildings were made

from brick. The new station finally opened on

December 17, 1900.

Soon, the island was made even bigger. A large

hospital was added, too.

A Long Trip

What was it like to come to America 100 years ago? The trip from Europe took two weeks. Families traveled across the Atlantic Ocean in big, crowded boats. They came from different countries. Some people became sick during their trip.

The boats came to New York City. Immigrants left their boats and got on a ferry. The ferry took them to Ellis Island. When they entered the station, they wondered what would happen next.

The Tests

Inside the station, the immigrants stood in lines. A doctor checked to see if they were sick. The doctor looked at their eyes, hands, and throats. Some people had to do puzzles to show how smart they were. Sick people went to the hospital. Some were sent back to Europe.

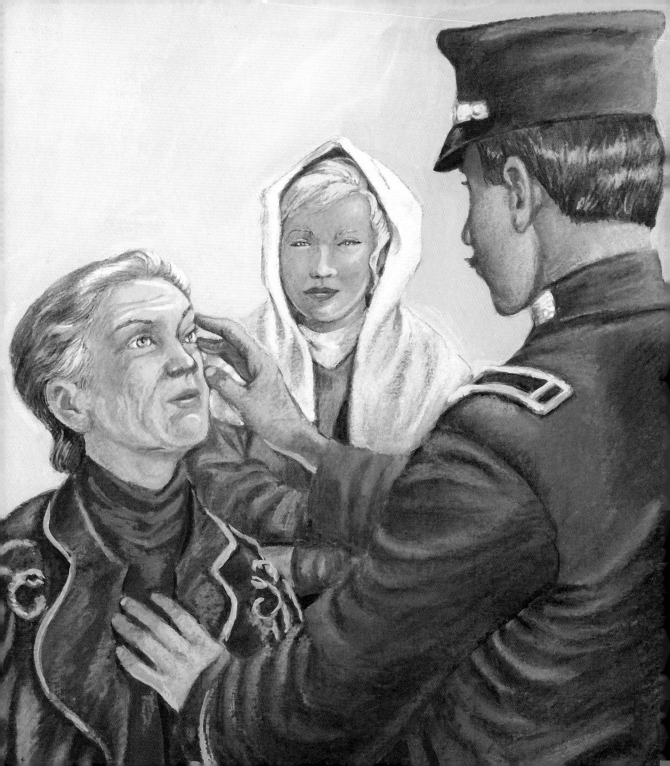

Important Questions

Next, immigrants came to the Great Hall.

The room was noisy. Babies cried. People spoke in

many languages.

The immigrants waited in long lines to speak

with clerks. The clerks decided who could stay in

the United States. The clerks asked many questions.

They wrote down the immigrants' names. They

made sure the immigrants had money. They asked

if the immigrants had a job to go to.

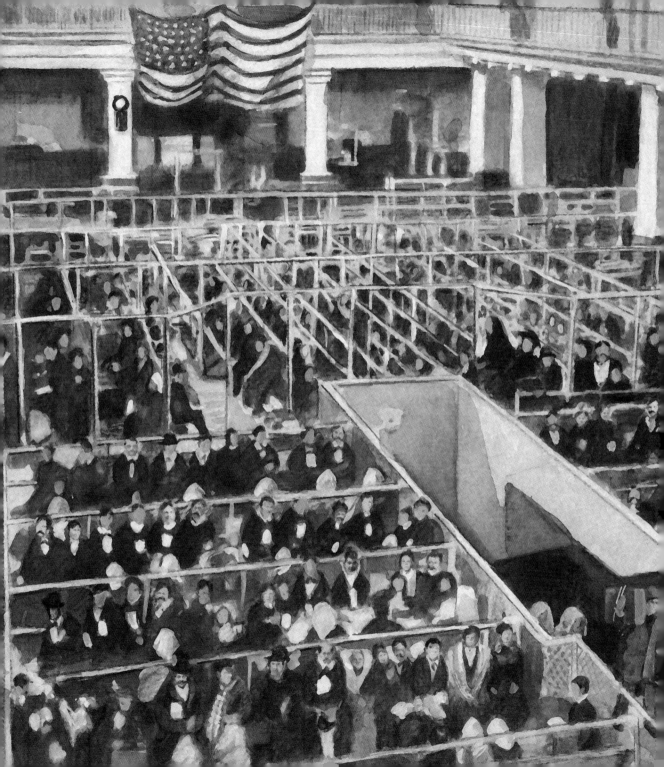

Welcome to America!

Most immigrants spent hours or even days on Ellis Island. Then they were let through. Their new lives in America could begin!

At the island, the immigrants got ready to live in the United States. They turned in money from their countries. In return, they got U.S. dollars worth the same amount. They bought train tickets to different cities. Then, they got their bags and took the ferry to the mainland.

The Station Closes

In the 1920s, new laws passed. Fewer people were allowed to move to the United States. The lines at Ellis Island grew shorter and shorter.

The station closed in 1954. It had been open for 62 years. The island was made into a national park in 1965. Today, immigrants to the United States come from around the world. They arrive in airplanes, boats, trains, and cars.

22

Ellis Island Today

The buildings on Ellis Island were left empty for years. Nobody took care of them, and they began to fall apart. After 30 years, the buildings were fixed. The main one became the Ellis Island Immigration Museum. It opened on September 10, 1990.

The museum shows how the station was used. It tells the stories of those who passed through it.

A Visit to Ellis Island

You can take a boat to visit Ellis Island. The boat stops in front of the museum.

In the museum, you can watch a movie about Ellis Island's history. You can explore the museum's three floors. Each room shows different parts of the station's history. You will learn what it was like for the immigrants who came to the station years ago.

What the Island Means

Ellis Island is an important national symbol. It is a reminder of the millions of immigrants who came to the United States. We celebrate the different cultures of American people today.

Fun Facts

- The busiest day for Ellis Island was April 17, 1907. On this day, 11,747 immigrants went through the station.

- More than 12 million immigrants went through the station in 62 years.

- Ellis Island is part of the park that includes the Statue of Liberty. You can see the Statue of Liberty from Ellis Island.

- The land on Ellis Island was made eight times bigger with sand and dirt. The original island was 3.3 acres (1.3 ha). Today, it is 27.5 acres (11.1 ha).

- There are 33 buildings on Ellis Island.

- The American Family Immigration History Center is also on Ellis Island. There, you can find out if someone in your family went through the station.

Glossary

clerk—a person who keeps records in an office.

culture—the ways of life of the people from a certain country.

ferry—a boat that brings people to and from a place every day.

fireproof—when something cannot be destroyed by fire.

immigrant—a person who leaves his or her home country to live in a new country.

symbol—something that stands for something else.

On the Web

To learn more about Ellis Island, visit ABDO Group online at **www.abdopublishing.com**. Web sites about Ellis Island are featured on our Book Links page. These links are routinely monitored and updated to provide the most current information available.

Index